YOUNG PROFILES

Mary-Kate
&
Ashley Olsen

Bailey J. Russell

ABDO Publishing Company

visit us at
www.abdopub.com

Published by ABDO Publishing Company, 4940 Viking Drive, Edina, Minnesota 55435.
Copyright © 2004 by Abdo Consulting Group, Inc. International copyrights reserved in
all countries. No part of this book may be reproduced in any form without written
permission from the publisher.

Printed in the United States.

Cover Photo: Corbis
Interior Photos: AP/Wide World, Corbis, Getty Images, Shooting Star

Editors: Kate A. Conley, Stephanie Hedlund, Kristianne E. Vieregger
Art Direction: Neil Klinepier

Library of Congress Cataloging-in-Publication Data

Russell, Bailey J., 1963-
    Mary-Kate & Ashley Olsen / Bailey J. Russell.
        p. cm. -- (Young profiles)
    Includes index.
    Summary: A simple biography of the twin Olsen sisters, who began their acting
careers sharing the role of a baby on the television series "Full House" and who today
produce and star in their own videos, CDs, and books.
    ISBN 1-59197-408-9
    1. Olsen, Ashley, 1986---Juvenile literature. 2. Olsen, Mary-Kate, 1986---Juvenile
literature. 3. Actors--United States--Biography--Juvenile literature. [1. Olsen, Ashley,
1986- 2. Olsen, Mary-Kate, 1986- 3. Actors and actresses. 4. Women--Biography.] I.
Title: Mary-Kate and Ashley Olsen. II. Title. III. Series.

PN2287.O36R87 2003
791.45'028'092273--dc21
    [B]
                                                                        2003042582

Contents

The Olsen Twins

Mary-Kate and Ashley Olsen are two of today's biggest celebrities. The talented twins have starred in four television series and several movies. They have also made hit videos and CDs.

Mary-Kate and Ashley rocketed to fame on the popular television series *Full House*. Fans have watched them grow from babies to teenagers, and their popularity is growing as fast as they are!

Mary-Kate and Ashley can do it all—television, movies, music, fashion, video games, dolls, and books. And, millions of loyal fans can't wait to see what the twins will do next.

Mary-Kate and Ashley have celebrity dolls by Mattel.

Mary-Kate (right) and Ashley Olsen

Profile of Mary-Kate Olsen

Mary-Kate Olsen

Name: Mary-Kate Olsen

Date of Birth: June 13, 1986—two minutes after Ashley

Place of Birth: Los Angeles, California

Parents: David and Jarnette Olsen, stepmother McKenzie

Siblings: Brother Trent, sisters Ashley and Elizabeth, half-sister Taylor, and half-brother Jake

Eyes: Blue-green

Hair: Blonde

Features: Left-handed, one inch shorter than Ashley, a round face with a freckle on her right cheek

Hobbies: Horseback riding, swimming, kickboxing, and basketball

Profile of Ashley Olsen

Ashley Fuller Olsen

Name: Ashley Fuller Olsen

Date of Birth: June 13, 1986–two minutes before Mary-Kate

Place of Birth: Los Angeles, California

Parents: David and Jarnette Olsen, stepmother McKenzie

Siblings: Brother Trent, sisters Mary-Kate and Elizabeth, half-sister Taylor, and half-brother Jake

Eyes: Blue-green

Hair: Blonde

Features: Right-handed, one inch taller than Mary-Kate, an oval face with a freckle above her lip

Hobbies: Dancing, tennis, kickboxing, golf, and swimming

Home and Family

Mary-Kate and Ashley Olsen were born on June 13, 1986. They are **fraternal** twins, not **identical**. So, though they seem exactly alike, they aren't! Mary-Kate is left-handed, while Ashley is right-handed. And, Ashley is a little taller than Mary-Kate.

The twins live in California. Their dad, David, is a mortgage banker. Their mom, Jarnette, was a professional dancer. David and Jarnette are divorced. David later remarried. His second wife's name is McKenzie.

Mary-Kate and Ashley have an older brother and a younger sister. Trent and Elizabeth have appeared in some of the twins' videos. Mary-Kate and Ashley also have two **siblings** from their father's second marriage, sister Taylor and brother Jake.

Opposite page: Mary-Kate and Ashley have some differences, even though it doesn't look like it at first!

Mary-Kate and Ashley attend a regular school when they
are not working on a television series or making movies.
When they are working, they study on location with a **tutor**.

Full House

When Mary-Kate and Ashley were seven months old, their mother took them to an **audition**. It was for a television show called *Full House*. The Olsen twins won the role of Michelle Tanner.

Mary-Kate and Ashley shared the role. That's because in California, labor laws **restrict** how much child actors can work. For this reason, television shows often hire twins for children's roles. That way, one child doesn't have to work too much.

The first **episode** of *Full House* aired on September 22, 1987. Bob Saget played Danny Tanner, a man whose wife had just died. Danny was trying to raise his three daughters. They were DJ, played by Candace Cameron, Stephanie, played by Jodie Sweetin, and Michelle, played by Mary-Kate and Ashley.

The cast of Full House

Danny needed help around the house and with his children. So, he asked his brother-in-law Jesse Katsopolis and his friend Joey Gladstone to live with him and the girls. Jesse was played by John Stamos, and Joey was played by Dave Coulier.

Great acting and good **scripts** made *Full House* a hit. The cute twins soon **upstaged** the talented, **veteran** actors. As the show's popularity grew, Mary-Kate and Ashley became well-known celebrities.

Full House was on television for eight seasons. The last **episode** aired on August 29, 1995. But, America couldn't get enough of the twins. Their fans waited to see what they would do next.

Opposite page: In this episode, Ashley (right) played Uncle Jesse's cousin from Greece.

Pint-Sized Producers

In 1993, Mary-Kate and Ashley formed their own production company. It is called Dualstar Entertainment. Dualstar is organized into different divisions that generate many different products.

With Dualstar, the twins can develop their own projects. As producers, Mary-Kate and Ashley call all the shots. They can do the projects they want to do, just like they want to do them. The twins read **scripts**, make casting choices, and select story ideas. "We love getting involved," Ashley said. "It's a complete blast."

Through Dualstar, Mary-Kate and Ashley began producing their own videos. In 1997, Dualstar was the number two company for top-selling videos. Only Disney sold more! Dualstar has been a huge success. The twins are not only talented entertainers, they are also skilled businesswomen!

Mary-Kate and Ashley became producers when they were seven years old. They're Hollywood's youngest producers ever!

Video Vault

Mary-Kate and Ashley's videos have been very successful. In September 1993, *Mary-Kate and Ashley: Our First Video* went to number one on *Billboard*'s music video chart in less than three weeks. It spent 12 weeks in the number one spot.

Mary-Kate and Ashley are the youngest performers to hit **quadruple platinum** and number one on *Billboard*'s charts. *Mary-Kate and Ashley: Our First Video* was one of the top 10 videos for 157 weeks!

The twins began producing two direct-to-video series. *The Adventures of Mary-Kate and Ashley* videos are mysteries. The twins play detectives called the Trenchcoat Twins who can "solve any crime by dinner time." The videos are fun and take place in unusual locations.

Mary-Kate (left) and Ashley appeared at the 2002 Hollywood Reporter's "Women In Entertainment: Power 100" breakfast.

In the second series, *You're Invited to Mary-Kate and Ashley's*, the twins have parties and the viewer is invited! The parties are held at places everyone loves to go, such as the mall and the beach.

The hit videos are musicals. And, through Dualstar Records, Mary-Kate and Ashley have released CDs and cassettes of their music.

Twins in Print

Through Dualstar Publications, Mary-Kate and Ashley publish books based on their hit videos and television shows.

Adventures of Mary-Kate and Ashley and the New Adventures of Mary-Kate and Ashley series are mystery stories. There are books based on the *You're Invited to Mary-Kate and Ashley's* series of party videos as well. The twins also published books that go with their television series *Two of a Kind.*

Mary-Kate and Ashley in It Takes Two

Mary-Kate and Ashley recently added a few new series to their book collection. They are Mary-Kate and Ashley Sweet 16, Mary-Kate and Ashley in ACTION!, So Little Time, and Starring In.

Mary-Kate and Ashley's books are as popular as their videos and CDs! Fans can't get enough of the twins' adventures. There are millions of Mary-Kate and Ashley's books in print, and a new book is released nearly every month.

Mary-Kate (left) and Ashley talk with publisher Robert J. Dowling at a Hollywood event.

Movie Stars

In 1992, Mary-Kate and Ashley began making television movies. That year, the twins released *To Grandmother's House We Go*. It was followed by *Double, Double, Toil and Trouble* in 1993. *How the West was Fun* and *The Little Rascals* were released in 1994.

The twins moved to the big screen with their first feature film, *It Takes Two*, in 1995. Mary-Kate and Ashley won

Mary-Kate and Ashley pose on the set of How the West was Fun.

Nickelodeon's Kids' Choice Award for Best Actresses of the Year in 1996 for their performances in *It Takes Two.*

The twins continued making movies. *Billboard Dad,* a feature-length film that went straight to video, was released in 1998. In 1999, *Switching Goals,* about two soccer-playing sisters, appeared on the Wonderful World of Disney. In 2003,

Mary-Kate (right) and Ashley Olsen

Mary-Kate and Ashley were in *Charlie's Angels: Full Throttle.* They had a **cameo** appearance as themselves.

Back to Television

In 1998, Mary-Kate and Ashley produced a new television series called *Two of a Kind*. In it, the twins played Mary-Kate and Ashley Burke. Christopher Sieber played the girls' dad. He was a college professor who hired one of his students, played by Sally Wheeler, to **supervise** Mary-Kate and Ashley while he was at work.

That same year, Mary-Kate and Ashley again won Nickelodeon's Kids' Choice Award for Best Actresses of the Year for their performances in *Two of a Kind*. But sadly, *Two of a Kind* was on for only one year.

In 2000, the twins produced a television special, "Behind the Walls of Full House." In this informative show, viewers were treated to highlights from *Full House* and interviews with cast members.

Mary-Kate (right) and Ashley in the hit show Two of a Kind.

In 2001, the twins produced a new television series, *So Little Time*. In it, the twins played Riley and Chloe Carlson. Clare Carey played their mother, and Eric Lutes played their father. Riley and Chloe's parents were separated, and the show focused on the challenges the twins faced at home, at school, and with friends.

For her performance as Riley, Mary-Kate was nominated for a Daytime Emmy Award for Outstanding Performer in a Children's Series. Though she did not win the award, the nomination was an acknowledgment of Mary-Kate's acting talent. *So Little Time* ended in 2002, after 26 popular **episodes**. *So Little Time* and *Two of a Kind* are both still played in **reruns**.

In 2002, the twins produced a new series. *Mary-Kate and Ashley in ACTION!* is a cartoon. It is on the Disney Channel. Mary-Kate and Ashley star as special agents fighting evil with the help of their robot dog.

Mary-Kate (right) and Ashley Olsen

Expanding Horizons

Mary-Kate and Ashley continue to demonstrate their remarkable business sense by developing products their fans want. Dualstar Interactive now produces video games geared toward girls for Sony PlayStation and Game Boy systems.

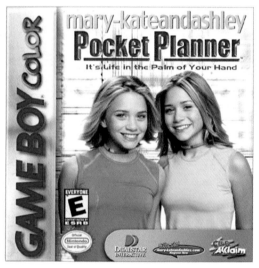

Mary-Kate and Ashley develop video games for girls!

In 2001, *mary-kateandashley* magazine hit newsstands. The magazine is popular with Mary-Kate and Ashley's fans. That same year, the twins launched a line of clothing. They were also named the Most Powerful Young Women in Hollywood by the *Hollywood Reporter*.

In 2002, Mary-Kate and Ashley presented the Breakthrough Video Award at the MTV Video Music Awards. That same year, they received the first DVD Premiere Franchise Performers Award. And, their 2002 movie *When in Rome* was nominated for Best Live Action DVD Premiere Movie of the Year.

The Olsen twins presenting MTV's Breakthrough Video Award

A Fabulous Future

Mary-Kate and Ashley Olsen are among the most popular celebrities in the entertainment industry today. On *Full House*, they were babies who shared a role. Through smart business decisions and hard work, the twins are now recognized as individually talented entertainers.

Mary-Kate and Ashley are working to expand their products worldwide. Their clothing line is sold in the United States, Canada, Australia, and the United Kingdom. Their Web site is popular with fans around the world as well.

In addition, the twins have taken a **hiatus** from their direct-to-video movies. This allows them to concentrate on feature films. With so many projects in the works and possibilities to explore, Mary-Kate and Ashley Olsen have a bright future.

Mary-Kate (right) and Ashley wave to fans.

Glossary

audition - a short performance to test someone's ability.

cameo - a small role usually performed by a well-known actor.

episode - one show in a series of shows.

fraternal - twins that are different from each other in some ways.

hiatus - a break.

identical - twins that are exactly alike.

quadruple platinum - when a video or album sells 4 million copies.

rerun - a movie or television show that is aired several times.

restrict - to keep within certain limits.

script - the text or words that actors say in a television show or a movie.

sibling - a brother or sister.

supervise - to watch over and take care of something.

tutor - a teacher who gives private lessons to students.

upstage - when an actor is more popular than other actors in a television show or movie.

veteran - a person with a lot of experience.

Web Sites

To learn more about Mary-Kate and Ashley, visit ABDO Publishing Company on the World Wide Web at **www.abdopub.com**. Web sites about the twins are featured on our Book Links page. These links are routinely monitored and updated to provide the most current information available.

Mary-Kate and Ashley Olsen

Index